ANIMALS

Sharks

by Kevin Holmes

Content Consultant:
Jammie Willey, Curator
Maine Aquarium

Bridgestone Books
an imprint of Capstone Press

Bridgestone Books are published by Capstone Press,
151 Good Counsel Drive, P.O. Box 669, Mankato, Minnesota 56002.
www.capstonepress.com

072011
006231CGVMI

Library of Congress Cataloging-in-Publication Data
Holmes, Kevin J.
　　Sharks/by Kevin J. Holmes.
　　p. cm.—(Animals)
　　Includes bibliographical references and index.
　　Summary: An introduction to sharks, covering their physical characteristics,
habits, prey, and relationship to humans.
　　ISBN-13: 978-1-56065-600-5 (hardcover)
　　ISBN-10: 1-56065-600-X (hardcover)
　　ISBN-13: 978-0-7368-8070-1 (paperback)
　　ISBN-10: 0-7368-8070-4 (paperback)
　　1. Sharks—Juvenile literature. [1. Sharks.] I. Title.
II. Series: Animals (Mankato, Minn.)
QL638.9.H65   1998
596.3—dc21

　　　　　　　　　　　　　　　　　97-12203
　　　　　　　　　　　　　　　　　CIP
　　　　　　　　　　　　　　　　　AC

Photo credits
Innerspace Visions/James D. Watt, 8; Amos Nachoum, 10; Michael
　Nolan, 14; Doug Perrine, 18
Kenneth J. Howard, cover, 4, 6, 16, 20
Visuals Unlimited/Marty Snyderman, 12

Table of Contents

Nostril

Eye

Gill
Slits

Dorsal
Fin

Mouth

Pectoral
Fins

Tail
Fin

Anal Fin

Pelvic
Fins

Fast Facts

Kinds: There are more than 350 kinds of sharks. Each shark has its own features.

Range: Sharks are fish that live in every ocean except the Arctic Ocean. The Arctic is too cold for sharks. Some sharks also live in freshwater lakes and rivers.

Habitat: All kinds of sharks live in water. Some sharks live in shallow water. Some sharks live in medium deep water. Other sharks are deep-dwellers. They live in very deep water.

Food: Many sharks eat animals such as crabs, fish, or squid. Some sharks eat tiny animals and plants.

Mating: Scientists do not know how wild sharks mate.

Young: Young sharks are called pups. Some pups hatch from eggs. Others are born from their mothers.

Sharks

Sharks are fish that live in every ocean except the Arctic. The Arctic is too cold for sharks. Some sharks also live in freshwater lakes and rivers.
There are more than 350 kinds of sharks. Each shark has its own features.

Most people believe sharks are killers. This is because sharks are predators. A predator hunts and eats other animals for food. But most sharks are not dangerous to people. Only 32 kinds of sharks are known to attack people.

Sharks breathe underwater with gills. A gill is an organ on a fish's side that helps it breathe. The surface of the gills is very thin. The gills take in oxygen from the water. Gills give sharks the oxygen they need to live. Sharks have five to seven gill openings. The openings are called slits.

People have skeletons made of bone. Sharks have cartilage skeletons. Cartilage is a strong, rubbery tissue. It helps sharks bend and swim easily.

Sharks breathe underwater with gills.

Appearance

Most sharks have rounded bodies that narrow at each end. This shape makes their bodies streamlined. Streamlined means shaped to move more quickly through the water.

Most sharks have two fins on their backs. These are called dorsal fins. Sharks also have one pair of pectoral fins on their sides. Pectoral fins help sharks steer and balance as they swim. Sharks also have pelvic fins and anal fins. These help sharks swim. Sharks have one tail fin. Tail fins help move sharks through the water.

A shark has nostrils near the tip of its snout. A snout is the long front part of an animal's head.

Sharks like the tiger shark are named for other animals. Sharks are also named for their colors. The great white shark was named for its color. Some sharks are named because they look like other objects. The head of a hammerhead shark looks like a hammer.

Hammerhead sharks have heads that look like hammers.

Strengths

A shark is a powerful predator. A shark's greatest strength is its powerful jaws. Some sharks can bite 300 times harder than people.

A shark's jaws are full of sharp teeth. A shark may have up to five sets of teeth at one time. The shark uses its front set for eating and hunting. After awhile, the shark's teeth become dull from eating. The old teeth fall out. A new set moves forward to replace the old teeth. A shark may use more than 29,000 teeth in a lifetime.

A young shark may grow a new set of teeth every week. An adult shark replaces its outer set of teeth seven to 12 times each year. This keeps the teeth sharp and ready for action.

A shark's skin is covered with scales. The scales help protect the shark. A shark's scales are sharp like teeth. The scales can cut people and other fish.

Sharks have several sets of teeth.

Hunting

Sharks are excellent hunters. They swim quickly toward prey. Prey is an animal that is hunted and eaten as food. Some sharks can swim up to 40 miles (64 kilometers) per hour.

Sharks' senses also help them hunt food. Sharks have excellent eyesight. Their eyes can see through dark and cloudy waters. Some sharks can see seven times better than people.

Sharks have special cells near their noses. These cells sense movements in the water.

Sharks also have powerful senses of smell. They smell with their nostrils and breathe with their gills. Sharks can smell other animals. Sharks also smell the blood of hurt animals. Blood often attracts sharks.

Blood in the water can start a feeding frenzy. A feeding frenzy is when a group of sharks loses control. The sharks wildly attack anything in the water. Sometimes they even attack other sharks.

Sharks use their nostrils to smell other animals.

Food

Different kinds of sharks prefer different foods. The kind of teeth sharks have depends on what food they eat. Most sharks have razor-sharp teeth. These teeth are used for eating animals such as fish and squid.

Some sharks eat crabs and sea animals with shells. These sharks have flat teeth. Sharks use their flat teeth to break the hard shells of the animals. Then they can eat them.

Other sharks eat mainly plankton and small fish. Plankton is the mix of tiny animals and plants found in ocean water. Sharks that eat plankton do not need sharp teeth.

Some sharks swallow anything that gets in their way. They even eat garbage. People have found clocks, old coats, jewelry, and tin cans inside sharks.

Many sharks eat fish.

Enemies

Most sharks have very few enemies. Only large ocean animals and people can harm sharks.

Killer whales, sperm whales, and large fish might attack smaller sharks. Sometimes larger sharks attack smaller sharks, too.

Porpoises might fight back if a shark attacks their young. Porpoises are sea animals that swim in groups. The porpoises take turns ramming a shark. Some sharks even die from these fights.

People sometimes put sharks in danger. Some people sell fish for a living. They sell the sharks' meat, oil, and fins. Some people eat shark-fin soup. Others use sharks for medicine. Some people catch sharks just for fun. People kill 20 million to 100 million sharks every year.

People pollute the water where sharks live. Pollution can hurt or kill sharks. Some scientists worry because so many sharks are dying. They fear that sharks might not exist in the future.

People sometimes catch sharks.

Young Sharks

Scientists do not know how most wild sharks mate. Few wild sharks have been observed while mating. Sharks can be born in three ways.

Some females lay eggs. The eggs are often inside leathery shells called mermaids' purses. The shells have string-like growths on them. These growths anchor the eggs to plants or rocks. The females leave the eggs. After time, the eggs hatch. The amount of time depends on the kind of shark. Young sharks are called pups. The pups then swim away.

Some females carry eggs inside their bodies. The eggs hatch inside the mother. The newborn pups eat the eggs and may eat each other. Only one or two pups are born from many eggs. Other sharks grow inside the mother's body. They are born live from their mothers. At birth, pups care for themselves. The mother may eat pups if they do not leave quickly.

Pups care for themselves once they are born.

Sharks and People

Sharks attack about 75 people each year. Most people are attacked in warm waters during the summer.

Many people are afraid of sharks. This is because they have heard about shark attacks. But most sharks will not attack people. More people die from bee stings than from shark attacks.

Sharks do not attack people for food. Sometimes they attack because they mistake people for food. They may attack people out of fear. Sometimes people swim too close to sharks. Sharks sense danger if people come too close.

Scientists are trying to find ways to protect people from sharks. They are learning from a fish called the moses sole. Sharks do not attack the moses sole. The moses sole sprays a chemical into an attacking shark's mouth. The chemical tastes bad to the shark. The shark swims away. Scientists are trying to make this chemical.

About 75 people are attacked by sharks each year.

Hands On: Mystery Food

Sharks are eating machines. Sharks find their prey through their sense of smell. How well can you smell? Play the following game to find out.

What You Need

10 or more different kinds of foods with strong smells
One handkerchief to use as a blindfold
One or more friends

What You Do

1. Blindfold a friend.
2. Pick some foods and hold them under your friend's nose. Can your friend guess what the food is?
3. Move the food farther away. Try to hold the food three feet (one meter) away from your friend's nose. How close does the food have to be before your friend can pick up the scent?
4. Take turns being blindfolded. See who can guess the most foods correctly.

Words to Know

cartilage (KAR-tuh-lij)—a strong, rubbery tissue

gill (GIL)—an organ on a fish's side that helps it breathe

plankton (PLANGK-tuhn)—the mix of tiny animals and plants that drift in the ocean

predator (PRED-uh-tur)—an animal that hunts another animal for food

snout (SNOUT)—the long, front part of an animal's head

streamlined (STREEM-lined)—shaped to move more quickly through the water

Read More

Arnold, Caroline. *Watch Out for Sharks!* New York: Clarion Books, 1991.

Behrens, June. *Sharks*. Chicago: Children's Press, 1990.

Useful Addresses

Sea World
Education Department
1720 South Shores Road
San Diego, CA 92109

Shark Education Network
Greenlife Society
700 Cragmont Avenue
Berkeley, CA 94708

Internet Sites

FactHound offers a safe, fun way to find Internet sites related to this book.

Go to *www.facthound.com*

He'll fetch the best sites for you!

Index